THE COMPLETE 5 - INGREDIENT COOKBOOK

Healthy, Delicious Recipes for Your Loved Ones.
Show Your Love, Care and Support to Each Family Member.

Keri Fox

Copyright 2022 by Keri Fox
All rights reserved.

TABLE OF CONTENTS

INTRODUCTION 1

CHAPTER 1: 5 INGREDIENT RECIPES 2

    Feeding a Family 2

    The 5-Ingredient Solution 2

CHAPTER 2: BREAKFAST 5

    Sweet Potato Toast 7

    Spicy Turmeric Egg Scramble 9

    Steel-Cut Oats with Banana, Cherries, and Almonds 11

    Quick Greens and Cauliflower Bowl 13

    Green Smoothie 14

    Mango-Almond Muesli 15

    Loaded Almond Butter and Avocado Toast 16

    Nutty Quinoa Granola 17

    Blueberry Smoothie Bowl 18

    Banana Oat Pancakes 19

    Blueberry Breakfast Muffins 21

    Spinach, Mushroom, and Egg White Omelet 23

CHAPTER 3: LUNCH 25

    Whitefish Chowder 27

    Sardine Salad 29

    Walnut Bean Burgers 30

    Sheet Pan Winter Vegetable Bake 32

    Homemade Avocado Sushi 34

Grilled Five-Spice Chicken Skewers 36

Walnut-Crusted Salmon Fillets 38

Lemony Salmon with Mixed Vegetables 40

Spicy Trout Sheet Pan Dinner 42

Pork Tenderloin with Warm Tomato Dressing 44

Smoky Coppa and Collard Greens 46

Sheet Pan Sausage, Pear, and Brussels Sprouts 48

Pan-Seared Pork Loin 50

Mushroom Beef Flax Meatballs 51

Heart-Healthy Meatloaf 52

Chicken Curry 53

Chicken, Mushroom, and Bell Pepper Skewers 55

CHAPTER 4: DINNER 57

Watermelon and Quinoa Salad with Feta and Mint 59

Quinoa Flatbread Pizza 61

Greek Pizza 63

Broccoli and Bean Casserole 65

Coconut Chicken Curry 67

Mediterranean Mackerel 69

Baked Salmon Patties with Greens 71

Spiced Trout and Spinach 73

Salmon Patties 75

Pork Verde Tacos 77

Banh Mi Pork 79

Sausage and Cabbage Skillet 81

Spinach and Sweet Potato Bacon Hash 83

Garlic Beef and Broccoli Stir-Fry 85

Walnut Pesto Beef Skewers 87
Turkey Meatballs 89
Lemon Chicken and Asparagus 90

CHAPTER 5: DESSERTS 93

Broiled Cinnamon Apple Crumble 95
Dark Chocolate Superfood Bark 96
No-Bake Pumpkin Almond Butter Energy Balls 98
Matcha Lime Coconut Ice Pops 99
Carrot Cake Bites 100
Chocolate Avocado Pudding 102
Blueberry-Yogurt Ice Pops 103
Chocolate Chia Seed Pudding 104
Almond Butter Freezer Fudge 105
Grain-Free Coconut Fruit Crisp 106
Chocolate Chia Pudding 107
Pumpkin Pie Pudding 108

CONCLUSION 109

INTRODUCTION

Although producing five-ingredient meals is not new, it has grown more popular than ever due to the increased pace of modern life. All of the recipes in this cookbook were chosen based on four criteria: they are simple to prepare, they require readily available ingredients, they are nutritious, and they are delicious. Every recipe in this book. Each recipe has only five ingredients for breakfast, lunch, dinner, and dessert. Cooking oil, salt, pepper, herbs, and water are not considered ingredients because they are frequently on hand and almost always required.

The whole family will love these easy-to-make meals, and the time you save on cooking will allow you to spend more time with your family at the table. As you cook through this book and realize how wonderful the recipes are, you will gain culinary confidence and the desire to prepare more family meals. Additionally, you will feel good about feeding your family because you will utilize nutritious, natural products. With each dish, full-color photographs and detailed instructions make it easier than ever to enjoy your favorite foods. Five ingredients may appear to be a small number at first glance; after all, what can you do with so few components?

Have no fear. You will see. Cooking with only five components requires less purchasing, fewer ingredients to stock, fewer opportunities for a mistake, less time for cleanup, and less time for preparation. As a beginner cook, it is easy to mix up measurements (was that a teaspoon or a tablespoon?). Keeping the ingredient lists brief will allow you to concentrate on the technique and quality of the dish rather than on keeping track of a hundred ingredients. This book was created to help you prepare healthy, delectable meals with minimal effort and inexpensive, readily available ingredients.

Prepare to unleash your cuisine's rich flavors and fragrant smells using only five ingredients. This cookbook is suitable for cooks of all skill levels, as it contains various recipes. It is a fundamental necessity for busy individuals. I hope the recipes and advice in this cookbook expand your dinner options and enable you to quickly prepare great, nutritious meals. Let's begin preparing recipes using five ingredients. Happy and wholesome cooking!

Chapter 1: 5 Ingredient Recipes

If you're not used to the kitchen, cooking might be a really scary experience. However, even a novice cook should be able to master the dishes presented in this cookbook. The dishes in this book are so good that most people can't believe they just require five ingredients each. As you work through this cookbook, you will undoubtedly feel more at ease in the kitchen and be inspired to cook more home-cooked meals for your loved ones. These recipes are aromatic and delicious. Because you are utilizing nutritious, natural products, you can feel good about what you are serving your family. It's a win-win situation!

To save time and effort in the kitchen, you can make one dish everyone enjoys by following the recipes in this cookbook, which call for common ingredients. Those with a full schedule would benefit from simple dishes that require even less time in the kitchen. Flavorful food can be made with little effort. A simple meal may be transformed into something spectacular by adding key components, such as olive oil, a spice blend, fresh herbs, and citrus.

Feeding a Family

How we provide for our families appears to undergo profound changes with each generation. Maybe you don't cook as many meals at home as your parents or grandparents did. Probably, you also rely more on convenience and processed foods. In a busy household, finding the time to prepare and serve healthy, nutritious meals consistently can be difficult. There is no more work to be done. More kids are participating in after-school activities, and more parents are working. People with many commitments may have trouble coordinating their calendars to eat simultaneously. In turn, this leads to having less time to cook and eat together as a family. Eating out is a convenient alternative to cooking dinner for many harried households. It might be discouraging to prepare nutritious meals from scratch when eating out or ordering takeout is so convenient.

The 5-Ingredient Solution

If you want to make cooking easier and more enjoyable, try cutting down on the number of ingredients. The benefits of 5 ingredient recipes:

Easy shopping: Who doesn't like a quick exit from the supermarket? This is even worse than squandering a ton of time and money at the grocery store by trying to carry too many items in your cart, which causes it to overflow. The worst part about bringing them home has to unloading them finally. Nothing of the sort will occur with these recipes.

Saving money: The cost of groceries and restaurants may mount up rapidly. If you budget your money in advance, you'll be able to eat whenever you want without going into debt. This gives you more freedom over what goes into your meals. You can afford to indulge a little while you're out.

Saving time: When compared to the time it takes to order and pick up takeout, some of these meals can be made in less time. or arrange for shipment and/or local pickup.

Better health: You can choose every ingredient when you cook at home. When dining at a restaurant, it's important to consider You can end up eating unhealthy meals if you rely on restaurants. Numerous other factors can accumulate over time and contribute to a decline in health.

Sense of accomplishment: It's rewarding to put your own hands to the task of preparing and enjoying a meal.

Chapter 2: Breakfast

SWEET POTATO TOAST

Time to prepare: 5 minutes / Cook time: 10 minutes • Serves 4

Ingredients

- Two medium sweet potatoes washed and cut into ¼-inch-thick slices
- 2 tablespoons extra-virgin olive oil, divided
- 3 or 4 chipotle peppers in adobo (from a 7.5-ounce can), plus more as needed
- 1 cup low-fat or nonfat Greek yogurt
- 1 cup fresh spinach, torn or chopped
- 8 large eggs, fried or poached

Method

1. Lightly brush each side of each slice of sweet potato with olive oil.
2. In a toaster or toaster oven on a medium-high setting, toast the slices. Cook them for 2 to 3 cycles or until soft.
3. Put 3 to 4 chipotle peppers in a food processor and pulse to mince. Alternatively, you may mince the peppers by hand. Reserve the can contents.

4. Add the yogurt to the food processor bowl (or use a separate bowl if mincing by hand). Stir to combine.
5. Taste and add more peppers or a tablespoon of the sauce from the can to increase the spice level.
6. To serve, plate the sweet potato slices and top with 1 tablespoon of sauce, about ¼ cup of spinach, 1 egg, and another 1 tablespoon of sauce on top.

Nutrition Info:

Per Serving (2 slices): Calories: 312; Total fat: 17g; Carbohydrates: 21g; Protein: 18g

SPICY TURMERIC EGG SCRAMBLE

Time to prepare: 10 minutes / Cook time: 10 minutes • Serves 2

Ingredients

- 2 teaspoons extra-virgin olive oil
- 4 large eggs, whisked
- ½ cup low-fat cottage cheese
- 2 garlic cloves, freshly minced and set aside for 10 minutes
- ½ teaspoon ground turmeric
- ¼ teaspoon cayenne pepper

Method

1. In a skillet, heat the olive oil over medium heat.
2. Add the eggs and cottage cheese and whisk to combine. Add the turmeric, garlic, and cayenne pepper, and whisk again.

3. Cook for 4 to 5 minutes, gently stirring occasionally to prevent browning on the bottom. When the eggs are set (liquid is mostly absorbed), remove the skillet from the heat. Sprinkle more pepper, if desired, and serve warm.

Nutrition Info:

Per Serving: Calories: 231; Total fat: 15g; Carbohydrates: 4g; Protein: 20g

STEEL-CUT OATS WITH BANANA, CHERRIES, AND ALMONDS

Time to prepare: 5 minutes / Cook time: 15 minutes • Serves 6

Ingredients

- 2 cups steel-cut oats
- 4½ cups unsweetened dairy-free milk
- 1 spotted large banana, fresh or frozen and thawed, sliced
- 2 cups tart cherries, fresh or frozen, halved and pitted
- ½ cup slivered almonds, chopped
- 1 tablespoon cinnamon (optional)

Method

1. In a large saucepan, combine the oats and milk and boil over medium-high heat. Reduce the heat. Simmer for 15 minutes or until the oats are soft.
2. Remove from the heat and add the banana. Cover the saucepan for 2 to 3 minutes to soften the banana.
3. Mash or stir the softened banana into the oats until incorporated. Add the cherries and almonds, mixing to combine.

4. Serve immediately, garnished with cinnamon (if using) and more cherries or almonds, if desired.

Nutrition Info:

Per Serving: Calories: 288; Total fat: 9g; Carbohydrates: 45g; Protein: 10g

QUICK GREENS AND CAULIFLOWER BOWL

Time to prepare: 5 minutes / Cook time: 5 minutes • Serves 1

Ingredients

- 4 kale leaves, thoroughly washed and chopped
- 1½ cups cauliflower florets
- ½ avocado, chopped
- 2 teaspoons lemon juice, or more to taste
- 1 teaspoon extra-virgin olive oil
- Pinch salt
- Pinch pepper

Method

1. Fill the pan with 2 inches of water and insert a steamer basket. Bring to a boil over high heat.
2. Put the kale and cauliflower in the basket. Cover and steam for 5 minutes.
3. Transfer the vegetables to a medium bowl. Toss with avocado, lemon juice, olive oil, salt, and pepper.

Nutrition Info:

Per Serving: Calories: Calories: 317; Total fat: 21g; Carbohydrates: 29g; Protein: 11g

GREEN SMOOTHIE

Time to prepare: 5 minutes • Serves 2

Ingredients

- 3 cups baby spinach
- Juice of 1 lemon
- ½ avocado
- 2 Granny Smith apples, cored and chopped
- ¼ cup cilantro leaves (optional)
- 1-inch piece of ginger, peeled
- 2 cups water
- 1 cup crushed ice

Method

1. In a blender, combine the spinach, lemon juice, avocado, apple, cilantro (if using), ginger, water, and ice. Blend until smooth.

Nutrition Info:

Per Serving: Calories: 199; Total fat: 8g; Carbohydrates: 30g; Protein: 3g

MANGO-ALMOND MUESLI

Time to prepare: 5 minutes / Cook time: 15 minutes • Serves 4

Ingredients

- 1½ cups rolled oats
- ½ cup sliced almonds
- ⅓ cup unsweetened dried coconut
- 1 tablespoon ground cinnamon
- ½ cup dried mango, cut into ½-inch pieces

Method

1. Preheat the oven to 350F. Prepare a baking sheet with parchment paper. In a bowl, coconut, combine the oats, almonds, and cinnamon. Spread the mixture out evenly on the lined baking sheet. Sprinkle the mango on top.
2. Bake for 15 minutes or until the oats are browning and the mango is soft and sticky. To serve warm, pour ½ cup of boiling water over ½ cup of muesli. To serve cold, add ½ cup of muesli to ½ cup of unsweetened plant-based milk. Serve.

Nutrition Info:

Per Serving (¼ recipe): Calories 295; Fat 14g; Protein 8g; Carbohydrates 36g

LOADED ALMOND BUTTER AND AVOCADO TOAST

Time to prepare: 2 minutes / Cook time: 2 minutes • Serves 2

Ingredients

- 2 slices whole-grain bread or gluten-free bread, toasted
- ¼ cup almond butter
- 1 avocado, pitted, peeled, and sliced
- 2 teaspoons honey
- Red pepper flakes
- Sea salt

Method

1. On each slice of toast, layer 2 tablespoons of almond butter and half the avocado. Drizzle 1 teaspoon of honey on top and sprinkle with red pepper flakes and salt.

Nutrition Info:

Per Serving: Calories: 443; Total fat: 33g; Carbohydrates: 32g; Fiber: 12g; Sugar: 10g; Protein: 12g

NUTTY QUINOA GRANOLA

Time to prepare: 10 minutes / Cook time: 25 minutes • Serves 4

Ingredients

- ½ cup peanut butter
- ¼ cup maple syrup
- 1 cup rolled oats
- 1 cup uncooked quinoa
- 1 cup whole raw almonds

Method

2. Preheat the oven to 350oF. Make sure a baking sheet has been lined with parchment paper. In a microwave-safe bowl, heat the peanut butter for 30 to 45 seconds until melted. Mix the peanut butter and maple syrup. Add the oats, quinoa, and almonds.
3. Spread the mixture out on the baking sheet. To flatten the mixture, use a spoon to press down. Bake for 15 minutes until the granola starts to form solid sections. Flip and stir slightly, then bake for 10 minutes or until golden.
4. Allow it to cool on the baking sheet. Serve.

Nutrition Info:

Per Serving (¾ cup): Calories 661; Fat 35g; Protein 22g; Carbohydrates 71g

BLUEBERRY SMOOTHIE BOWL

Time to prepare: 10 minutes / Cook time: 0 minutes • Serves 2

Ingredients

- 1 cup fresh berries (such as strawberries, blueberries, or blackberries), plus more
- for topping
- 1 banana
- ½ cup low-fat plain Greek yogurt
- ½ cup low-fat milk
- 1 tablespoon crushed almonds

Method

1. In a blender, place the berries, banana, yogurt, and milk and
2. blend until smooth. Pour the smoothie into a bowl. Then top with crushed
3. almonds and fresh berries.

Nutrition Info:

Per Serving (1): Calories: 140; Total fat: 2g; Protein: 6g; Total carbohydrate: 26g

BANANA OAT PANCAKES

Time to prepare: 5 minutes / Cook time: 20 minutes • Serves 7

Ingredients

- 1 cup steel-cut oats
- 1 banana
- 1 large egg
- ½ cup low-fat milk (or plant-based alternative)
- 2 teaspoons baking powder
- Olive oil

Method

1. In a blender, place the oats, banana, egg, milk, and baking powder until smooth, about 20 seconds. Place a skillet over medium heat and coat it with olive oil.
2. Using 14-cup measurements, add the batter to the hot skillet to form 4 pancakes. Cook the pancakes until the edges turn slightly golden, about 2 minutes. Then flip

and cook for 2 minutes more on the other side. Repeat with the remaining batter. Serve immediately.

Nutrition Info:

Per Serving: (1 pancake): Calories: 143; Total fat: 3g; Protein: 5g; Total carbohydrate: 23g

BLUEBERRY BREAKFAST MUFFINS

Time to prepare: 10 minutes / Cook time: 20 minutes • Serves 9

Ingredients

- Olive oil
- 2 bananas
- 1 cup steel-cut oats
- 1 large egg
- 1 teaspoon baking powder
- ½ cup fresh blueberries

Method

1. Preheat the oven to 350°F. Lightly oil 9 cups of a muffin tin with oil. In a bowl, mash the bananas with a fork until smooth. Mix in the oats, egg, and baking powder until well combined.

2. Gently fold the blueberries into the mixture. Equally, divide the batter into the 9 prepared muffin cups and bake for 20 minutes. Remove the muffins from the oven. Cool and serve.

Nutrition Info:

Per Serving (1 Muffin): Calories: 112; Total fat: 2g; Protein: 3g; Total carbohydrate: 21g

SPINACH, MUSHROOM, AND EGG WHITE OMELET

Time to prepare: 10 minutes / Cook time: 5 minutes • Serves 2

Ingredients

- 2 cups chopped fresh spinach
- ½ cup diced white mushrooms
- 2 tablespoons water
- 1 tablespoon minced garlic
- Pinch salt
- 1 teaspoon olive oil divided
- 1½ cups liquid egg whites, divided

Method

1. In a skillet, place the spinach, mushrooms, water, garlic, and salt, and cook for about 2 minutes until fragrant. Transfer the vegetable mixture to a bowl.
2. Heat half the olive oil in the skillet. Cook ¾ cup egg whites for about 3 minutes or until firm. Use a spoon to scoop half of the vegetable mixture onto one side of the omelet and fold it over.

3. Transfer the omelet to a plate. Then repeat with the remaining olive oil, egg white, and vegetable mixture. Serve immediately.

Nutrition Info:

Per Serving (1 omelet): Calories: 132; Total fat: 3g; Protein: 22g; Total carbohydrate: 4g;

Chapter 3: Lunch

WHITEFISH CHOWDER

Ingredients

Time to prepare: 10 minutes / Cook time: 35 minutes • Serves 6

- 4 carrots, peeled and cut into ½-inch pieces
- 3 (peeled and cut into ½-inch pieces) sweet potatoes
- 3 cups full-fat coconut milk
- 2 cups water
- 1 teaspoon celery seed or ground thyme (optional)
- 1 teaspoon salt
- 1 teaspoon freshly ground black pepper
- 10½ ounces whitefish, skinless and firm, such as barramundi, cut into chunks
- Grated zest of 1 lime
- Juice of 3 limes
- ¼ cup minced parsley (optional)

Method

1. In a large stockpot, combine the carrots, sweet potatoes, coconut milk, water, celery seed (if using), salt, and

2. pepper. Bring to a boil. Then reduce the heat to low. Cover, and simmer for 20 minutes.
3. Put half the soup in a blender and puree it. Return the puree to the stockpot. Add the fish chunks.
4. Cook for 13 to 15 minutes or until the fish is tender and hot. Add the lime zest and juice and stir. Garnish with parsley (if using) and serve hot.

Nutrition Info:

Per Serving (1⅔ cup): Calories: 336; Total fat: 24g; Carbohydrates: 22g; Protein: 11g

SARDINE SALAD

Time to prepare: 10 minutes • Serves 4

Ingredients

- 2 (4¼-ounce) cans of sardines packed in olive oil, drained
- ¼ cup soy-free mayonnaise
- 2 tablespoons Dijon mustard
- 2 tablespoons diced pickles
- ½ teaspoon dried dill
- Freshly ground black pepper
- 2 (white and green parts, chopped) scallions (optional)
- Bread, mini sweet peppers, cucumber slices, or veggie dippers for Serving

Method

1. Put the drained sardines in a medium bowl and mash with a fork. Stir in the mayonnaise, mustard, pickles, dill, pepper, and scallions (if using).
2. Serve on bread, in lettuce cups, stuffed into mini sweet peppers, on top of cucumber slices, or with veggie dippers such as carrot or celery sticks.

Nutrition Info:

Per Serving (¼ cup): Calories: 122; Total fat: 10g; Carbohydrates: 1g; Protein: 7g

WALNUT BEAN BURGERS

Time to prepare: 10 minutes / Cook time: 25 minutes • Serves 4

Ingredients

- ¼ cup shredded carrots
- ¼ onion, any color
- 2 tablespoons chopped walnuts
- 1 tablespoon extra-virgin olive oil
- 1–2 teaspoons adobo seasoning (see headnote)
- 1 garlic clove, minced (optional)
- 1 tablespoon hot sauce (optional)
- 1 (15-ounce) (drained and rinsed) can of low-sodium black beans,

Method

1. Preheat the oven to 400F. Line a baking sheet with parchment paper.
2. In a food processor bowl, combine the carrots, onion, walnuts, oil, seasoning, garlic (if using), and hot sauce (if using). Pulse until evenly mixed and onions are minced.

Then add the black beans and pulse once or twice to incorporate. You still want to see pieces of black beans.
3. Scoop about ¼ cup of the mixture onto the baking sheet and press lightly to make a patty shape. Repeat with the remaining mixture until all the patties are formed. The mixture will be soft and moist. They will firm up in the oven the longer they bake.
4. Bake for about 10 minutes, flip, then bake for another 10 minutes. When the patties are firm enough to pick up, they are done. Do not overbake them.

Nutrition Info:

Per Serving (1 burger): Calories: 148; Total fat: 6g; Carbohydrates: 18g; Protein: 7g

SHEET PAN WINTER VEGETABLE BAKE

Time to prepare: 10 minutes / Cook time: 35 minutes • Serves 4

Ingredients

- 1 red onion, quartered
- 2 cups chopped root vegetables
- 1 cup halved cherry tomatoes
- 2 tablespoons balsamic vinegar
- 1 tablespoon extra-virgin olive oil
- 1 tablespoon honey
- 1 tablespoon minced rosemary, oregano, or both (optional)
- ½ teaspoon salt
- ½ teaspoon freshly ground black pepper
- 1 (10½-ounce) can of lentils, drained and rinsed (optional)

Method

1. Preheat the oven to 400°F. Line a sheet pan with parchment paper. Spread the onion, root vegetables, and tomatoes on the prepared sheet pan, toss with vinegar, oil, honey, herbs (if using), salt, and pepper, and mix well.
2. Bake for 40 to 45 minutes, stirring the vegetables halfway through to ensure even cooking. If using lentils, add them in the last 10 minutes of baking.

Nutrition Info:

Per Serving (1 cup): Calories: 96; Total fat: 4g; Carbohydrates: 16g; Protein: 1g

HOMEMADE AVOCADO SUSHI

Time to prepare: 20 minutes / Cook time: 15 minutes • Serves 4

Ingredients

- 3 cups water, plus additional for rolling
- 1½ cups dry quinoa, rinsed
- ½ teaspoon salt
- 6 nori sheets
- 3 avocados, halved, pitted, and sliced thin, divided
- 1 small cucumber, halved, seeded, and cut into matchsticks, divided
- Tamari or coconut aminos for dipping (optional)

Method

1. In a saucepan set over high heat, combine the water, quinoa, and salt and boil. Lower the heat to low, cover, and simmer for 15 minutes. Remove from the heat, fluff the quinoa and set aside.
2. On a cutting board, lay out 1 nori sheet. Spread ½ cup of quinoa over the sheet, leaving 2 to 3 inches uncovered at the top.

3. Place 5 or 6 avocado slices across the bottom of the nori sheet (the side closest to you) in a row. Add 5 or 6 cucumber matchsticks on top.
4. Starting at the bottom, tightly roll up the nori sheet. Dab the uncovered top with water to seal the roll.
5. Slice the sushi roll into 6 pieces. Repeat with the remaining 5 nori sheets, quinoa, and vegetables. Serve with tamari if using.

Nutrition Info:

Per Serving: Calories: 557; Total fat: 33g; Carbohydrates: 57g; Protein: 13g

GRILLED FIVE-SPICE CHICKEN SKEWERS

Time to prepare: 15 minutes, plus 30 minutes to chill / Cook time: 20 minutes • Makes 8 skewers

Ingredients

- 1 tablespoon extra-virgin olive oil
- 1½ tablespoons five-spice blend
- 2 tablespoons tamari or coconut aminos
- 1 cup fresh pineapple, bite-size pieces, some juice reserved
- 1 pound chicken thighs (boneless, skinless), cut into 1-inch pieces
- ½ red onion, chopped into large sections
- 16 garlic cloves (optional)
- 2 jalapeño peppers, quartered (optional)

Method

1. In a casserole dish, combine the olive oil, a five-spice blend, tamari, and 2 tablespoons of pineapple juice. Add the chicken, stir to coat it evenly, and put it in the fridge for 30 minutes to marinate.

2. Preheat the oven to 350°. Skewer the chicken, pineapple, onion, garlic (if using), and jalapeno (if using) in an alternating pattern until all ingredients are used (making 8 skewers).
3. Reserve the marinade liquid. Preheat an outdoor grill to medium heat. Place the skewers on the grill. Then brush with the remaining marinade, and close the lid. Grill for about 8 minutes, turning once or twice to prevent burning and ensure even cooking. Cool slightly, taste, sprinkle more five-spice, soy sauce, or tamari, if desired, then serve.

Nutrition Info:

Per Serving (2 skewers): Calories: 201; Total fat: 8g; Carbohydrates: 8g; Protein: 24g

WALNUT-CRUSTED SALMON FILLETS

Time to prepare: 10 minutes / Cook time: 20 minutes • Serves 4

Ingredients

- 1 tablespoon extra-virgin olive oil, divided
- 1 pound skin-on salmon fillet
- ½ cup walnuts, finely chopped
- 6 chive stalks, minced
- 1 teaspoon sea salt
- 1 teaspoon dried dill
- 1 tablespoon freshly squeezed lemon juice

Method

1. Preheat the oven to 350°F. Then line your baking sheet with parchment paper or foil. Brush half of the oil on all sides of the salmon and place skin-side down on the baking sheet.

2. Mix the walnuts, chives, salt, and dill in a small bowl. Stir in the lemon juice and the remaining ½ tablespoon olive oil. Gently press the mixture onto the top side of the salmon fillet. Bake for about 10 to 12 minutes or until the salmon is cooked.
3. Carefully transfer the salmon to plates to keep the topping in place.

Nutrition Info:

Per Serving: Calories: 262; Total fat: 17g; Carbohydrates: 2g; Protein: 26g

LEMONY SALMON WITH MIXED VEGETABLES

Time to prepare: 10 minutes / Cook time: 15 to 20 minutes • Serves 4

Ingredients

- 4 (5-ounce) wild salmon fillets
- 1 teaspoon salt divided
- 1 teaspoon black pepper, divided
- 2 lemons, 1 washed and sliced thin, and 1 quartered
- 1 broccoli head, coarsely chopped
- 1 cauliflower head, coarsely chopped
- 1 small bunch (4 to 6) carrots, cut into coins
- 1 tablespoon fresh herbs such as thyme and chopped parsley (optional)

Method

1. Preheat the oven to 400°F. Line a baking sheet with parchment paper. Place the fillets on the prepared sheet and sprinkle with ½ teaspoon each of salt and pepper.
2. Drape each fillet with a few lemon slices. Bake for 15 minutes or until the salmon is opaque and flakes easily with a fork. While the salmon cooks, fill a saucepan with

three inches of water and insert a steamer basket. Bring to a boil over high heat. Add the broccoli, cauliflower, and carrots to the saucepan.
3. Cover and steam for 6 to 8 minutes or until they are fork-tender. Sprinkle with ½ teaspoon of salt and pepper. Top each salmon fillet with a heaping pile of vegetables, a sprinkle of fresh herbs (if using), and a squeeze of fresh lemon, and serve.

Nutrition Info:

Per Serving: Calories: 330; Total fat: 13g; Carbohydrates: 20g; Protein: 35g

SPICY TROUT SHEET PAN DINNER

Time to prepare: 5 minutes / Cook time: 20 minutes • Serves 5

Ingredients

- 3 tablespoons minced garlic, divided
- 2 tablespoons chili powder, divided
- 2 tablespoons olive oil, divided
- Sea salt
- 1-pound rainbow trout fillets
- 2 zucchinis, sliced into rounds

Method

1. Preheat the oven to 425F. Line a baking sheet with parchment paper. Mix 2 tablespoons of garlic, 1 tablespoon of oil, 1 chili powder, and a pinch of salt. Generously coat both sides of the trout fillets with the garlic mixture and place them on one half of the baking sheet.
2. Mix the remaining garlic, chili powder, olive oil, and another pinch of salt in another medium bowl. Add the zucchini to the bowl. Then stir to combine. Bake the fish for 20 minutes until slightly browned on the edges. Add the zucchini to the empty side of the baking sheet halfway through the cooking time. Enjoy immediately.

Nutrition Info:

Per Serving (3 ounces of Trout and ½ cup zucchini): Calories: 186; Total fat: 9g; Protein: 20g; Total carbohydrate: 6g;

PORK TENDERLOIN WITH WARM TOMATO DRESSING

Time to prepare: 15 minutes / Cook time: 20 minutes • Serves 4

Ingredients

- 3 garlic cloves
- 1 pound pork tenderloin
- 4 teaspoons extra-virgin olive oil, divided
- 1¼ teaspoons salt, divided
- ½ teaspoon freshly ground black pepper
- 1 pint (10 ounces) cherry tomatoes
- ⅔ cup dry red wine
- ¼ cup balsamic vinegar
- 1 tablespoon sugar (optional)
- 1 teaspoon red wine vinegar (optional)

Method

1. Preheat the oven to 400F. Mince the garlic and let rest for 10 minutes. Brush the tenderloin with 1 teaspoon of oil and season with 1 teaspoon salt and pepper. Heat a skillet, add 1 teaspoon of oil and sear the pork on all sides for 3 to 4 minutes.

2. Roast for about 15 minutes or until the pork reaches 45F. In a pan, cook the remaining 2 teaspoons olive oil and the tomatoes, often stirring, until the tomatoes are blistered, about 5 minutes. Stir in the red wine, balsamic vinegar, and garlic, and cook for about 5 minutes or until the liquid is reduced by half.
3. Add the remaining ¼ teaspoon of salt, the sugar (if using), and the red wine vinegar (if using), and cook for about 1 more minute. Let the sauce cool slightly and spoon over the tenderloin before serving.

Nutrition Info:

Per Serving: Calories: 233; Total fat: 8g; Carbohydrates: 6g; Protein: 24g

SMOKY COPPA AND COLLARD GREENS

Time to prepare: 15 minutes / Cook time: 55 minutes • Serves 6 (½ cup)

Ingredients

- 2 garlic cloves
- 4 ounces coppa (Italian dry-aged meat) chopped
- 1 tablespoon extra-virgin olive oil
- 16 ounces chopped collard greens (about 12 cups)
- 2 cups water
- 2 large (both white and green parts) leeks, sliced
- ¼ cup red wine vinegar
- 1 teaspoon salt
- Hot sauce for Serving (optional)

Method

1. Mince the garlic and set aside for 10 minutes. In a pan, add the coppa and cook until crispy, about 5 minutes. Add the olive oil and garlic and sauté for 2 to 3 minutes.
2. Stir in the collards, water, leeks, vinegar, and salt. Cover and simmer for 42 to 45 minutes until the greens and leeks have softened. Serve with hot sauce (if using) or more salt and vinegar if desired.

Nutrition Info:

Per Serving: Calories: 137; Total fat: 9g; Carbohydrates: 9g; Protein: 8g

SHEET PAN SAUSAGE, PEAR, AND BRUSSELS SPROUTS

Time to prepare: 10 minutes / Cook time: 35 minutes • Serves 4

Ingredients

- 1 pound Brussels sprouts, trimmed and halved
- 3 shallots, quartered
- 2 firm-ripe pears, cored, cut into wedges
- 6 thyme sprigs
- 1 tablespoon extra-virgin olive oil
- ½ teaspoon salt
- ½ teaspoon freshly ground black pepper
- 1 pound bratwurst, or 4 links
- ¼ cup sauerkraut (optional)
- Dijon or spicy brown mustard for Serving (optional)

Method

1. Preheat the oven to 400F. Line a baking sheet with parchment paper. Spread the Brussels sprouts, shallots, pears, thyme, and oil on the prepared baking sheet, using your hands to coat everything evenly.
2. Sprinkle with salt and pepper. Then mix again. Arrange the bratwurst on top of the vegetables. Bake for 25 to 30 minutes. Remove the baking sheet from the oven. Distribute the sauerkraut over the vegetables (if using) and mix lightly. Serve warm with mustard (if using).

Nutrition Info:

Per Serving: Calories: 418; Total fat: 29g; Carbohydrates: 27g; Fiber: 7g; Sugar: 12g; Protein: 16g

PAN-SEARED PORK LOIN

Ingredients

Time to prepare: 15 minutes / Cook time: 35 minutes • Serves 8

- 1 cup water
- 1 (3-pound) boneless pork loin roast
- 2 tablespoons extra-virgin olive oil
- 1½ teaspoons salt
- 1 tablespoon fresh, finely minced
- ½ teaspoon freshly ground black pepper

Method

1. Preheat the oven to 375F. Pour the water into a 9-by-13-inch roasting pan. Heat a large skillet over high heat. Coat the roast with the olive oil and place it in the hot skillet.
2. Brown on all sides for about 2 to 3 minutes per side. Transfer the browned roast to the roasting pan. Combine the salt, rosemary, and pepper in a bowl and sprinkle the seasonings evenly over the meat.
3. Roast until the meat reaches 150F, about 30 to 35 minutes. Rest and serve.

Nutrition Info:

Per Serving (4½ ounces): Calories: 242; Total fat: 14g; Carbohydrates: 0g; Protein: 27g

MUSHROOM BEEF FLAX MEATBALLS

Time to prepare: 15 minutes / Cook time: 15 minutes • 4 to 6 servings

Ingredients

- 1 pound 90% lean grass-fed ground beef or ground sirloin
- 3 ounces mushrooms, minced
- 3 tablespoons garlic marinara
- 1 tablespoon ground flaxseed
- 1 tablespoon Italian seasoning
- 1 tablespoon nutritional yeast (optional)
- ½ teaspoon salt
- ¼ teaspoon freshly ground black pepper

Method

1. Preheat the oven to 400F. Cover a baking sheet with parchment paper. In a medium bowl, combine the ground beef, mushrooms, marinara, flaxseed, Italian seasoning, nutritional yeast (if using), salt, and pepper, and mix until just combined.
2. Scoop a heaping tablespoon of meat into the palm of your hands and roll it into a ball. Place on the baking sheet and repeat until all the meat mixture is used, making about 20 meatballs. Brush each meatball with oil and bake for 15 minutes. Cool slightly before serving.

Nutrition Info:

Per Serving: Calories: 216; Total fat: 12g; Carbohydrates: 2g; Protein: 24g

HEART-HEALTHY MEATLOAF

Time to prepare: 5 minutes / Cook time: 55 minutes • 5 servings

Ingredients

- 1-pound lean ground beef
- 1 cup whole-grain bread crumbs
- ¾ cup tomato Sauce, divided
- 1 large egg
- ½ white onion, diced

Method

1. Preheat the oven to 350F. Line a baking sheet with parchment paper. In a bowl, combine bread crumbs, the beef, ½ cup Tasty Tomato Sauce, egg, and onion.
2. Form a loaf with the ground beef mixture. Then and place it on the prepared baking sheet. Spread the rest of the sauce on top of the meatloaf and bake for 55 minutes, or until it reaches 160F. Serve immediately.

Nutrition Info:

Per Serving: (3 ounces): Calories: 269; Total fat: 7g; Protein: 24g; Total carbohydrate: 27g;

CHICKEN CURRY

Time to prepare: 5 minutes / Cook time: 15 minutes • 5 servings

Ingredients

- 1 tablespoon olive oil
- 1-pound boneless, skinless chicken thighs, thinly sliced
- 1 tablespoon minced garlic
- 1 white onion, diced
- 2 tablespoons curry powder
- ½ cup fat-free plain Greek yogurt
- Pinch sea salt

Method

1. Heat the oil and sauté the chicken and garlic in a skillet for approximately 10 minutes or until the chicken is thoroughly cooked. Add the onion and simmer for approximately 5 minutes or until transparent. Add the curry powder and stir for 1 to 2 minutes until it is fragrant.
2. Remove the skillet from the heat. Then stir in the yogurt and season with a pinch of salt. Serve immediately. Serving tip: Add some chopped cilantro on top to add color and another burst of flavor.

Nutrition Info:

Per Serving (3 ounces): Calories: 160; Total fat: 7g; Protein: 20g; Total carbohydrate: 4g

CHICKEN, MUSHROOM, AND BELL PEPPER SKEWERS

Time to prepare: 10 minutes / Cook time: 17 minutes • 4 servings

Ingredients

- 1-pound skinless, boneless chicken breast cut into 1-inch cubes
- ⅓ cup Oregano-Thyme Sauce
- 2 bell peppers, cut into 1-inch chunks
- 24 whole white mushrooms
- 1 tablespoon minced garlic
- 1½ tablespoons olive oil
- Sea salt

Method

1. Preheat the oven to 450°F. Line a baking sheet with parchment paper. Toss the chicken breast with the Oregano-Thyme Sauce. In another medium bowl, toss the peppers and mushrooms with garlic, olive oil, and a pinch of salt.
2. Thread the chicken, peppers, and mushrooms onto 8 skewers. (Ensure that wooden skewers are soaked for thirty minutes before use.) Place the skewers on the baking

sheet and bake for about 17 minutes, until the chicken edges are slightly brown and cooked to an internal temperature of 165F. Serve immediately.

Nutrition Info:

Per serving (2 skewers): Calories: 191; Total fat: 7g; Protein: 24g; Total carbohydrate: 8g;

Chapter 4: Dinner

WATERMELON AND QUINOA SALAD WITH FETA AND MINT

Time to prepare: 10 minutes / Cook time: 25 minutes • Serves 4

Ingredients

- 2 cups water
- 1 cup quinoa, rinsed
- 1 teaspoon salt
- ¼ cup extra-virgin olive oil
- 2 tablespoons freshly squeezed lemon juice
- 2 cups seeded watermelon, cut into ½-inch dice
- ½ cup crumbled sheep's or goat's milk feta cheese
- ¼ cup finely chopped fresh mint
- ¼ teaspoon freshly ground black pepper

Method

1. In a large stockpot, combine the water, quinoa, and salt. Bring to a boil. Then lower the heat, and simmer, partially covered, until all the water has been absorbed, 15 to 20 minutes. Remove it from the heat, let it cool to room temperature, and fluff it with a fork.
2. Add the oil and lemon juice and mix well. Add the watermelon and gently mix until just combined. Sprinkle the cheese, mint, and pepper over the salad and serve.

Nutrition Info:

Per Serving: Calories: 353; Total fat: 20g; Carbohydrates: 35g; Protein: 9g

QUINOA FLATBREAD PIZZA

Time to prepare: 10 minutes, plus 8 hours to soak / Cook time: 40 minutes • Makes 1 (8-inch) thick-crust flatbread or 2 thin crusts

Ingredients

- ¾ cup dry quinoa, rinsed
- 1¾ cups water, divided
- ½ teaspoon baking powder
- ½ teaspoon salt
- 2 tablespoons extra-virgin olive oil, divided
- 1 cup marinara or pasta sauce
- 1 cup sliced mushrooms
- 2 cups arugula
- 1 teaspoon red pepper flakes (optional)
- 6 slices fresh mozzarella or ½ cup shredded (optional)

Method

1. In a glass container, combine the quinoa and 1½ cups water and soak for 8 hours or overnight. Rinse and drain.
2. Preheat the oven to 425F. Line s pie pan (or two pans for two thin crusts) with parchment paper.

3. In a blender, combine the quinoa, the remaining ¼ cup water, the baking powder, the salt, and 1 tablespoon of oil and blend until creamy.
4. Pour the mixture into the prepared pan. If making 1 thick crust, bake for 20 minutes, flip, and then bake for another 10 minutes before removing for toppings. If making two thin crusts, bake for 20 minutes, then remove for toppings.
5. Remove the pan, brush the crust with the remaining 1 tablespoon olive oil, and add toppings of marinara, mushrooms, arugula, and red pepper flakes (if using). Tear and scatter the mozzarella (if using). Put the pizza back in the oven and bake for 10 minutes. Cool the pizza slightly before slicing and serving.

Nutrition Info:

Per Serving (¼ of thick pizza): Calories: 181; Total fat: 13g; Carbohydrates: 13g; Protein: 4g

GREEK PIZZA

Time to prepare: 15 minutes / Cook time: 25 minutes • Serves 5

Ingredients

- 1½ cups whole wheat or whole-grain self-rising flour, plus more for dusting
- 1 cup low-fat plain Greek yogurt
- 1½ cups Spinach and Walnut Pesto
- 1 tomato, thinly sliced
- ½ cup thinly sliced white mushrooms

Method

1. Preheat the oven to 350°F. Line a baking sheet with parchment paper. In a medium bowl, place the flour. Mix in the yogurt ¼ cup until the dough is smooth. Knead it into a ball.
2. Sprinkle 1 or 2 tablespoons of flour onto a cutting board or hard, clean surface, and form the dough ball into a 12-inch circle. Transfer the dough to the baking sheet and spread it evenly with the Spinach and Walnut Pesto. Arrange the tomato and mushrooms on top of the sauce.

3. Bake, the pizza crust for 25 minutes, or until the crust is golden brown. Enjoy immediately.

Nutrition Info:

Per Serving (⅕ pizza) Calories: 433; Total fat: 31g; Protein: 10g; Total carbohydrate: 33g

BROCCOLI AND BEAN CASSEROLE

Time to prepare: 10 minutes / Cook time: 35 to 40 minutes • Serves 4

Ingredients

- ¾ cup water or vegetable broth
- 2 medium broccoli heads, crowns, and stalks finely chopped
- 2 teaspoons pinto bean seasoning (or all-purpose seasoning blend)
- ½ teaspoon salt
- 1½ cups cooked pinto or navy beans, or 1 (14-ounce) can be drained
- 1 to 2 tablespoons brown rice flour or arrowroot flour
- 2 teaspoons nutritional yeast (optional)
- 1 cup walnuts, chopped
- ¼ cup salsa (optional)

Method

1. Preheat the oven to 350F. In a large ovenproof pot set on medium heat, warm the water. Add the broccoli, seasoning mix, and salt, and cook for 6 to 8 minutes or until the broccoli is bright green.
2. Stir in the beans, brown rice flour, and nutritional yeast (if using). Cook for about 5 minutes more or until the liquid thickens slightly. Sprinkle the walnuts over the top.

3. Bake for 20 to 25 minutes. The walnuts should be toasted. Serve with your favorite salsa if desired.

Nutrition Info:

Per Serving: Calories: 410; Total fat: 20g; Carbohydrates: 43g; Fiber: 13g; Protein: 22g

COCONUT CHICKEN CURRY

Time to prepare: 8 minutes / Cook time: 35 minutes • Serves 6

Ingredients

- 3 cups canned coconut milk
- 2 cups water
- 3 tablespoons curry powder
- 1 tablespoon garam masala (optional)
- 2 (boneless, skinless, cut into cubes) pounds chicken thighs
- 1 white onion, chopped
- 1 teaspoon salt
- 3 bunches of Swiss chard, washed, stemmed, and coarsely chopped
- 1 (15-ounce) can of chickpeas, drained and rinsed (optional)

Method

1. In a large saucepan, combine the coconut milk, water, curry powder, garam masala (if using), chicken, onion, and salt.

2. Bring to a boil. Then reduce the heat to low. Cover, and simmer for 30 minutes. Add the Swiss chard and chickpeas (if using) to the saucepan. Cook for 5 minutes or until the chard wilts and the chickpeas are warm.

Nutrition Info:

Per Serving (without chickpeas): Calories: 581; Total fat: 40g; Carbohydrates: 10g; Protein: 48g

MEDITERRANEAN MACKEREL

Time to prepare: 10 minutes / Cook time: 20 minutes • Serves 4

Ingredients

- 4 (4-ounce) cans of mackerel fillets, drained
- 1½ cups cherry tomatoes
- 2 tablespoons dry white wine
- 8 garlic-stuffed olives, halved (optional)
- Grated zest and juice of 1 lemon
- Freshly ground black pepper
- Salt
- 6 thyme or oregano sprigs (optional)
- 4 cups arugula (optional)

Method

1. Preheat the oven to 350F. In a casserole dish, arrange the fillets. Add the tomatoes, white wine, and olives (if using) to the top and sides. Sprinkle with lemon zest and juice, pepper, salt, and fresh herbs (if using).

2. Bake for 18 to 20 minutes or until the cherry tomatoes have burst and the fish starts to crisp up on the edges. Serve over a bed of 1 cup arugula (if desired).

Nutrition Info:

Per Serving (without chickpeas): Calories: 369; Total fat: 21g; Carbohydrates: 13.2g; Protein: 29.7g

BAKED SALMON PATTIES WITH GREENS

Time to prepare: 15 minutes / Cook time: 35 To 38 minutes • Serves 4

Ingredients

- 2 cups baked, mashed sweet potatoes (about 2 large sweet potatoes)
- 2 (6-ounce) cans of wild salmon, drained
- ¼ cup almond flour
- ¼ teaspoon ground turmeric
- 2 tablespoons olive oil
- 2 kale bunches, thoroughly washed, stemmed, and cut into ribbons
- ¼ teaspoon salt

Method

1. Preheat the oven to 350°F. Line a baking sheet with parchment paper. In a bowl, stir together the mashed sweet potatoes, salmon, almond flour, and turmeric.
2. Using a ⅓-cup measure, scoop the salmon mixture onto the prepared baking sheet. Flatten gently using the measuring cup's bottom. Repeat with the remaining mixture.

Bake the patties for 30 minutes, turning them halfway through. Heat the oil in a skillet set over medium heat.
3. Add the kale and sauté for 5 to 8 minutes, until the kale is bright and wilted. Sprinkle with salt. Serve with the salmon patties.

Nutrition Info:

Per Serving: Calories: 320; Total fat: 13g; Carbohydrates: 32g; Protein: 21g

SPICED TROUT AND SPINACH

Time to prepare: 10 minutes / Cook time: 15 minutes • Serves 4

Ingredients

- Extra-virgin olive oil for brushing
- ½ red onion, thinly sliced
- 1 (10-ounce) package of frozen spinach, thawed
- 4 boneless freshwater trout fillets
- 1 teaspoon salt
- ¼ teaspoon chipotle powder (optional)
- ¼ teaspoon garlic powder
- 2 tablespoons freshly squeezed lemon juice

Method

1. Preheat the oven to 375°F. Brush a 9-by-13-inch baking pan with olive oil. Scatter the red onion and spinach in the pan and lay the trout fillets on the spinach.

2. Sprinkle the fish with salt, chipotle powder (if using), and garlic powder, cover with foil, and bake until the Trout is firm, about 15 minutes. Drizzle with lemon juice and serve.

Nutrition Info:

Per Serving: Calories: 160; Total fat: 7g; Carbohydrates: 5g; Protein: 19g

SALMON PATTIES

Time to prepare: 20 minutes / Cook time: 40 minutes • Serves 5

Ingredients

- ¼ cup quinoa, rinsed
- ½ cup water
- 2 (7½-ounce) cans of low-sodium deboned salmon packed in water
- 1 tablespoon mustard
- 1 teaspoon Old Bay Seasoning
- 2 large eggs
- Olive oil

Method

1. Bring quinoa and water to a boil in a pan over high heat. Turn the heat down to low. Then simmer until the liquid is absorbed, about 20 minutes. Remove from the heat, fluff with a fork, and let cool. Preheat the oven to 400F.
2. Line a baking sheet with parchment paper. Mix the salmon, mustard, and seasoning in a bowl until well combined. Add the quinoa and eggs and combine well, then

shape the mixture into 5 patties. The patties should be baked for 20 minutes or until they begin to brown on the edges. Serve hot.

Nutrition Info:

Per serving (1 patty): Calories: 202; Total fat: 10g; Protein: 23g; Total carbohydrate: 6g

PORK VERDE TACOS

Time to prepare: 10 minutes / Cook time: 35 minutes • Serves 4

Ingredients

- 1 teaspoon salt
- ½ teaspoon black pepper
- 1 teaspoon ground cumin
- 1 pound pork tenderloin
- 1 tablespoon olive oil
- 1 (16-ounce) jar tomatillo (green) salsa, divided
- 8 (6-inch) grain-free or corn tortillas
- ½ cup freshly prepared guacamole
- 1 cup fresh spinach, chopped (optional)
- ½ bunch of cilantro, chopped (optional)
- 1 jalapeño pepper, chopped (optional)

Method

1. Preheat the oven to 325F. Sprinkle the salt, pepper, and cumin on all sides of the pork. The oil should be heated over medium heat in a pot with a lid (or a Dutch oven).

2. Add the pork. Sear it on all sides. Add the salsa (reserve ¼ cup for topping) and stir to coat the pork evenly. Bring back to a simmer, then cover, transfer the whole pot to the oven and cook for 30 to 35 minutes.
3. Slice or shred, and serve warm in tortillas topped with 1 tablespoon guacamole, 1 tablespoon salsa, spinach (if using), cilantro (if using), and jalapeño pepper (if using).

Nutrition Info:

Per Serving (2 tacos): Calories: 363; Total fat: 13g; Carbohydrates: 35g; Fiber: 7g; Protein: 29g

BANH MI PORK

Time to prepare: 15 minutes, plus 30 minutes to 1 day to chill / Cook time: 10 minutes. Serves 6

Ingredients

- 2 tablespoons fish sauce
- 1 tablespoon extra-virgin olive oil, divided
- 1 tablespoon rice vinegar
- 1 tablespoon honey
- 2 garlic cloves, minced
- 1 teaspoon salt
- ½ teaspoon black pepper
- 1 pound pork tenderloin, thinly sliced
- Two cups pickled vegetables, divided (optional;)
- ¼ cup sauerkraut, divided (optional)
- ¼ cup chopped cilantro, divided (optional)
- Sriracha (optional)

Method

1. Mix the fish sauce, oil, vinegar, honey, garlic, salt, and pepper in a medium glass bowl. Stir in the pork, cover, and chill for 30 minutes daily. Thread the pork onto skewers. Meanwhile, mince the garlic and set aside for about 10 minutes.
2. Heat an indoor or outdoor grill to medium heat. Place the skewers on the grill. Then brush with the remaining marinade, and close the lid. Grill for about 8 minutes, turning once or twice to prevent burning and ensure even cooking.
3. Cool slightly. Divide the pork among the bowls. Top with pickled vegetables (if using) and optional toppings of choice.

Nutrition Info:

Per Serving: Calories: 125; Total fat: 5g; Carbohydrates: 3g; Protein: 16g

SAUSAGE AND CABBAGE SKILLET

Time to prepare: 15 minutes / Cook time: 25 minutes • 4 to 6 servings

Ingredients

- 4 garlic cloves divided
- 1 tbsp. Plus 1 tsp. extra-virgin olive oil, divided
- 12 ounces smoked 100% grass-fed beef sausage, sliced
- 1 yellow onion, diced
- 1 cabbage (large head green) cored and coarsely chopped
- 2 large carrots, peeled and chopped
- 1 teaspoon salt
- ½ teaspoon freshly ground black pepper
- 1 tablespoon red wine vinegar (optional)

Method

1. Mince the garlic and set aside for 10 minutes. Heat 1 teaspoon of oil in a skillet with a lid. Stir in the sausage. Then cook until browned, 3 to 5 minutes. Transfer the sausage (keeping the drippings) from the skillet onto a paper towel-lined plate.

2. Reduce the heat to low. Add the remaining 1 tablespoon of oil, and sauté the onion for 3 minutes or until softened. Add half of the garlic and sauté for another 1 to 2 minutes. Stir in the cabbage, carrots, salt, and pepper.
3. Cover and cook for about 10 minutes until the cabbage and carrots have softened. Uncover and add the remaining garlic and red wine vinegar (if using). Cook for another 2 to 3 minutes. Serve hot and season with more salt or pepper to taste.

Nutrition Info:

Per Serving: Calories: 332; Total fat: 17g; Carbohydrates: 32g; 15g; Protein: 16g

SPINACH AND SWEET POTATO BACON HASH

Time to prepare: 10 minutes / Cook time: 20 minutes • Serves 4

Ingredients

- 6 bacon slices
- 1 (10-ounce) package of frozen chopped spinach
- ¼ cup water
- 2 medium sweet potatoes, cubed
- 1 small red onion, chopped
- 2 tablespoons extra-virgin olive oil
- ½ teaspoon salt
- ¼ teaspoon freshly ground black pepper
- ½ cup sauerkraut (optional)
- Hot sauce for Serving (optional)

Method

1. Heat a skillet over medium-high heat. Put in the bacon, and cook for about 3 minutes. Then flip and cook for another 3 minutes or until mostly crispy. Transfer the bacon to a plate. Discard the grease, and lightly wipe out the skillet with a paper towel.

2. Return the skillet to medium-high heat and put in the spinach and water. Cook until the moisture is absorbed and the spinach is thawed/warmed, about 5 minutes. Transfer the spinach to one side of the plate with the bacon.
3. Put the sweet potato, onion, and oil in the empty skillet, and stir. Cook for 10 minutes on low heat, covered. Stir occasionally. After 5-10 minutes of covered cooking, uncover, toss, and check the potatoes for doneness. Add the spinach, bacon, salt, and pepper. Stir and cook until all components are heated through. Serve hot, topped with the sauerkraut (if using) and a drizzle of hot sauce (if using).

Nutrition Info:

Per Serving: Calories: 224; Total fat: 13g; Carbohydrates: 18g; Fiber: 4g; Sugar: 4g; Protein: 10g

GARLIC BEEF AND BROCCOLI STIR-FRY

Time to prepare: 15 minutes / Cook time: 20 minutes • Serves 4

Ingredients

- 5 garlic cloves
- 2 medium heads of broccoli, chopped
- 1 tablespoon extra-virgin olive oil
- 3 tablespoons tamari, plus more for Serving
- 1 pound flank steak, thinly sliced
- 1 (1-inch) piece ginger, peeled and minced
- ½ teaspoon freshly ground black pepper
- 2 scallions, green and white parts, sliced, for Serving (optional)
- 1 tablespoon sesame seeds for Serving (optional)
- Sriracha, for Serving (optional)

Method

1. Mince the garlic and set aside for 10 minutes. In the meantime, bring 1 inch of water to a simmer in a pan with a steamer attachment over medium-high heat. Add the broccoli and cover to steam until bright green and al dente, about 5 minutes.
2. Heat a skillet and add the oil and tamari. Cook for 2 to 3 minutes until bubbly and reduced a bit. Add the beef and sauté until nearly done, about 5 minutes. Add the garlic, ginger, steamed broccoli, and pepper.
3. Cook for 2 to 3 minutes until the garlic is softened and aromatic and the beef is cooked. Taste and add more tamari, pepper, or salt as desired. Serve hot and sprinkle with scallions (if using), sesame seeds (if using), or sriracha (if using).

Nutrition Info:

Per Serving: Calories: 344; Total fat: 14g; Carbohydrates: 24g; Protein: 34g

WALNUT PESTO BEEF SKEWERS

Time to prepare: 15 minutes / Cook time: 20 minutes • Makes 8 skewers

Ingredients

- 1 pound flank steak, cut into 1-inch pieces
- ¼ cup olive or avocado oil, divided
- 3 tablespoons red wine vinegar divided
- ¾ teaspoon salt, divided
- ¼ teaspoon freshly ground black pepper
- ½ teaspoon red pepper flakes, divided (optional)
- 1 cup fresh basil
- 2 tablespoons chopped walnuts
- 1 garlic clove
- 1 tablespoon water
- 1 tablespoon nutritional yeast (optional)

Method

1. In a large glass dish, combine the steak pieces, 1 tablespoon of oil, 1 tablespoon of vinegar, ½ teaspoon of salt, the black pepper, and ¼ teaspoon of red pepper flakes (if using).
2. Stir well to evenly coat, cover, and refrigerate for 30 minutes up to 1 hour to help tenderize the meat. Heat a grill to medium heat and lightly oil the grates. Thread the

beef on 8 skewers. Place on the grill and close the lid. Grill for about 8 minutes, turning once or twice to prevent burning.
3. Puree the basil, remaining 2 tablespoons of vinegar, the walnuts, the garlic, water, 3 tablespoons of oil, remaining ¼ teaspoon of salt, the nutritional yeast (if using), and the remaining ¼ teaspoon of red pepper (if using). Cool slightly, top with pesto, and serve.

Nutrition Info:

Per Serving (2 skewers): Calories: 277; Total fat: 19g; Carbohydrates: 1g; Protein: 25g

TURKEY MEATBALLS

Time to prepare: 5 minutes / Cook time: 15 minutes • Makes about 20 meatballs

Ingredients

- 1-pound lean ground turkey
- 1½ cups Spinach and Walnut Pesto
- ½ cup whole-grain bread crumbs
- 1 large egg
- ½ white onion, finely diced

Method

1. Preheat the oven to 375°F. Line a baking sheet with parchment paper. In a medium bowl, mix the turkey, Spinach and Walnut Pesto, bread crumbs, egg, and onion until well combined.
2. With your hands, form the mixture into about 20 (1½-inch) meatballs. Spread the meatballs out on a baking sheet. Bake for 15 minutes or until the meat reaches 165F. Serve immediately.

Nutrition Info:

Per Serving (3 meatballs): Calories: 440; Total fat: 37g; Protein: 17g; Total carbohydrate: 10g

LEMON CHICKEN AND ASPARAGUS

Time to prepare: 5 minutes / Cook time: 20 minutes • Serves 5

Ingredients

- 1-pound boneless, skinless chicken thighs cut into 1-inch pieces
- ½ cup Lemon-Garlic Sauce
- 2½ cups (about 1 pound) chopped asparagus
- 1 tablespoon minced garlic
- 1½ tablespoons olive oil
- Sea salt
- Freshly ground black pepper

Method

1. To marinate the chicken, combine it with the lemon-garlic sauce in a resealable plastic bag, and chill it for at least 30 minutes. In a medium bowl, toss the asparagus with the garlic and olive oil and season with salt and pepper.

2. In a skillet over high heat, sauté the chicken until cooked and browned, about 15 minutes. Place the chicken on a platter and set it aside. Add the asparagus to the skillet and sauté until tender-crisp, about 5 minutes. Enjoy immediately.

Nutrition Info:

Per Serving (3 ounces of chicken and ½ cup asparagus): Calories: 221; Total fat: 13g; Protein: 20g; Total carbohydrate: 6g

Chapter 5: Desserts

BROILED CINNAMON APPLE CRUMBLE

Time to prepare: 10 minutes / Cook time: 3 minutes • Serves 4

Ingredients

- 3 large Granny Smith apples, cored and sliced thick
- 2 tablespoons salted butter, melted
- 1 tablespoon honey
- 2 tablespoons oats, pulsed into crumbs or finely chopped
- ½ teaspoon cinnamon

Method

1. Prepare the oven for broiling. Line a baking sheet with parchment paper. Spread apple slices in a single layer.
2. Mix the melted butter, honey, oats, and cinnamon in a bowl. Spread the mixture onto each apple slice. Broil for 2 to 3 minutes until the topping becomes golden and caramelized.
3. Transfer to a cooling rack, cool for 1 to 2 minutes, then enjoy warm.

Nutrition Info:

Per Serving: Calories: 167; Total fat: 6g; Carbohydrates: 27g; Protein: 1g

DARK CHOCOLATE SUPERFOOD BARK

Time to prepare: 10 minutes, plus 15 minutes to chill / Cook time: 5 minutes • Serves 16

Ingredients

- 16 ounces dark chocolate (70% cacao or above), broken into pieces
- 1 tablespoon sweetener of choice (allulose, maple syrup, honey, coconut sugar, etc.)
- ½ cup chopped nuts and seeds (cashews, almonds, pistachios, pumpkin seeds, etc.)
- ½ cup dried fruit (goji berries, candied ginger, cranberries, cherries, apricots, etc.)
- 1 handful of coconut flakes
- 1 teaspoon sea salt

Method

1. Line a baking sheet with parchment paper. The bottom pot of a double boiler should be filled with water to a depth of about 2 inches, and the top pot should be placed back inside. Combine the chocolate and sweetener in the top pot/bowl. Bring the water to a simmer over medium-low heat and stir to encourage melting.
2. When the majority of the chocolate has melted, usually after 4 to 5 minutes, remove it from the heat. Continue stirring until the chocolate is smooth. Pour the chocolate evenly on the prepared baking sheet. Sprinkle the nuts, seeds, dried fruit, coconut flakes, and sea salt over the chocolate.

3. Refrigerate the baking sheet for 1 hour or freeze for 15 minutes. Once the bark has cooled completely and is hard, break it into pieces using your hands. Serve or refrigerate for up to 1 week or freeze for up to 1 month.

Nutrition Info:

Per Serving (1 ounce): Calories: 214; Total fat: 15g; Carbohydrates: 18g; Protein: 3g

NO-BAKE PUMPKIN ALMOND BUTTER ENERGY BALLS

Time to prepare: 10 minutes, plus 30 minutes to chill • Makes 12 balls

Ingredients

- ½ cup canned pureed pumpkin (not pie filling)
- ⅓ cup creamy almond butter
- 3 tablespoons ground flaxseed
- 2 tablespoons allulose (or granule sweetener of choice)
- 1 teaspoon ground cinnamon

Method

1. In a food processor, combine the almond butter, pumpkin, flaxseed, sweetener, and cinnamon and process until smooth. Alternatively, add all the ingredients to a medium bowl and manually mix.
2. Chill the bowl in the refrigerator for 15 minutes. Using a spoon or small scooper, scoop about a tablespoon of the mixture into your hands and roll it into a ball. Repeat until all the dough is used.

Nutrition Info:

Per Serving (1 ball): Calories: 56; Total fat: 4g; Carbohydrates: 3g; Protein: 2g

MATCHA LIME COCONUT ICE POPS

Time to prepare: 10 minutes, plus 4 hours to chill • Serves 6

Ingredients

- 1 (14-ounce) can of full-fat coconut milk
- 4 scoops vanilla protein powder
- 6 tablespoons granule sweetener of choice
- 2 teaspoons matcha powder
- Juice of 2 limes
- 1 scoop spirulina (optional)

Method

1. In a blender, protein powder, combine the coconut milk, sweetener, matcha powder, lime juice, and spirulina (if using) and blend until smooth.
2. Taste and adjust sweetness, lime, and matcha as desired. Pour the mixture into ice pop molds. Then freeze for at least 4 hours. Allow sitting at room temperature for about 5 minutes before removing from molds.

Nutrition Info:

Per Serving (½ cup): Calories: 207; Total fat: 14g; Carbohydrates: 10g; Protein: 13g

CARROT CAKE BITES

Time to prepare: 10 minutes / Cook time: 10 minutes • Makes about 12 bites

Ingredients

- 1 cup quick-cooking oats divided
- 1 large egg
- ¼ cup golden raisins, divided
- 2 tablespoons hot water
- ⅛ teaspoon salt
- 1 teaspoon cinnamon
- ½ cup packed finely shredded carrots
- 2 tablespoons coconut butter or manna, melted (optional)

Method

1. Preheat the oven to 375°F. Line a baking sheet with parchment paper. In a small food processor, pulse ½ cup oats to make oat flour. Then add the egg, 2 tablespoons of golden raisins, the hot water, the salt, and the cinnamon.

2. Pulse until well combined and the egg is whisked. Transfer the contents to a medium bowl and mix the remaining ½ cup of oats, 2 tablespoons of golden raisins, and the carrots. Using a heaping tablespoon or 1-ounce scoop, scoop portions onto the prepared baking sheet, making about 12 bites.
3. Bake the cookies for 11 to 12 minutes or until golden brown. Remove the carrot cake bites from the oven and let them cool slightly. Drizzle with the melted coconut butter (if using) and serve.

Nutrition Info:

Per Serving: Calories: 147; Total fat: 3g; Carbohydrates: 26g; Protein: 6g

CHOCOLATE AVOCADO PUDDING

Time to prepare: 10 minutes, plus 1 hour to chill • Makes about 2 cups

Ingredients

- 10 Medjool dates, pitted
- 2 avocados, halved and pitted
- ½ cup cacao powder
- ¾ cup unsweetened flax or plant-based milk divided

Method

1. In a food processor, combine the avocados, dates, cacao powder, and ½ cup of milk. Blend until smooth.
2. If the pudding is too thick, add the remaining ¼ cup of milk and blend well. Refrigerate for 1 hour before serving.

Nutrition Info:

Per Serving (½ cup): Calories: 488; Total fat: 36g; Carbohydrates: 48g; Protein: 6g

BLUEBERRY-YOGURT ICE POPS

Time to prepare: 15 minutes, plus 2 hours to freeze • Serves 6

Ingredients

- 1 cup fresh blueberries
- Grated zest and juice of ½ lime, divided
- 1½ cups unsweetened yogurt or dairy-free alternative
- 2 tablespoons maple syrup, honey, or allulose
- ¼ teaspoon cinnamon

Method

1. In a bowl, mash the blueberries and add the lime zest. Divide the blueberry mixture among 6 ice pop molds.
2. Mix together the yogurt, lime juice, sweetener, and cinnamon in a bowl. Pour the yogurt mixture over the blueberries into the ice pop molds. Freeze until solid.

Nutrition Info:

Per Serving: Calories: 186; Total fat: 14g; Carbohydrates: 16g; 12g; Protein: 2g

CHOCOLATE CHIA SEED PUDDING

Time to prepare: 5 minutes, plus 5 hours to chill • Serves 5

Ingredients

- 1½ cups unsweetened plant-based milk
- ¼ cup chia seeds
- 2 tablespoons unsweetened cocoa powder
- 2 tablespoons maple syrup or 3 tablespoons allulose
- 1 teaspoon pure vanilla extract

Method

1. Whisk the milk, chia seeds, cocoa powder, maple syrup, and vanilla in a bowl. The cocoa may take 1 to 2 minutes to incorporate; keep whisking until no lumps remain. Cover the bowl. Refrigerate it for 30 minutes.
2. Stir the mixture after removing it from the refrigerator. Refrigerate it for another 30 minutes, and then stir it to ensure the mixture sets evenly. Leave the bowl in the refrigerator for 4 hours until the mixture has a thick, pudding-like consistency.
3. Serve immediately.

Nutrition Info:

Per Serving: Calories: 178; Total fat: 9g; Carbohydrates: 21g; Protein: 7g

ALMOND BUTTER FREEZER FUDGE

Time to prepare: 5 minutes / Cook time: 5 minutes • Makes 16 squares

Ingredients

- ¾ cup almond butter
- ⅓ cup coconut oil
- ¼ cup nonnutritive sweeteners, such as allulose or monk fruit
- ¼ teaspoon salt

Method

1. Use parchment paper to line a 9-by-5-inch loaf pan. In a small saucepan on low heat, combine the almond butter, coconut oil, sweetener, and salt.
2. Warm gently for about 5 minutes or until everything is incorporated. Pour the fudge into the prepared pan, smoothing it evenly with a spatula, and refrigerate for 1 hour. Slice the fudge into 16 squares and serve.

Nutrition Info:

Per Serving (1 square): Calories: 123; Total fat: 11g; Carbohydrates: 6g; Protein: 2g

GRAIN-FREE COCONUT FRUIT CRISP

Time to prepare: 5 minutes / Cook time: 30 to 35 minutes • Serves 6

Ingredients

- 3 cups mixed berries (raspberries, blueberries, blackberries, etc.)
- ¾ cup unsweetened shredded coconut
- ½ cup sunflower or pumpkin seeds
- ¼ cup granulated sugar or allulose
- ¼ cup coconut oil

Method

1. Preheat the oven to 350F. Spread the fruit in a 9-inch square baking dish. Mix the coconut, sunflower seeds, and sugar in a small bowl.
2. Stir in the coconut oil and incorporate it throughout using your hands. Crumble the topping over the fruit and bake for 32 to 35 minutes or until the fruit is bubbling.

Nutrition Info:

Per Serving: Calories: 379; Total fat: 29g; Carbohydrates: 29g; Protein: 4g

CHOCOLATE CHIA PUDDING

Time to prepare: 5 minutes plus 4 hours soaking time • Serves 2

Ingredients

- 1 cup of low-fat milk
- ½ cup chia seeds
- 2 tablespoons cocoa powder
- 1 tablespoon maple syrup
- 1 tablespoon vanilla extract

Method

1. Combine the milk, chia seeds, cocoa powder, maple syrup, and vanilla extract in a bowl.
2. Let the mixture stand for 12 to 15 minutes, stir again, and divide it between 2 Mason jars or lidded containers. Seal and refrigerate for 4 hours or overnight.

Nutrition Info:

Per Serving (½ cup): Calories: 383; Total fat: 19g; Protein: 14g; Total carbohydrate: 41g

PUMPKIN PIE PUDDING

Time to prepare: 10 minutes, plus 2 hours chilling time/ Cook time: 5 minutes • Serves 4

Ingredients

- 1 tablespoon gelatin
- ¼ cup water
- 1 (12-ounce) can of low-fat evaporated milk
- ½ cup pumpkin puree
- 1 tablespoon maple syrup
- 2 teaspoons cinnamon

Method

1. In a bowl, sprinkle the gelatin over the water and set aside for 10 minutes. In a pan over medium heat, stir together the evaporated milk, pumpkin puree, maple syrup, and cinnamon.
2. Heat for about 5 minutes or until it begins to foam. Take the pumpkin mixture off the stove and add the gelatin while it's still warm. Pour the pumpkin pie pudding through a fine sieve into four small (½-cup) ramekins, cover with plastic wrap, and refrigerate for 2 hours. Serve chilled.

Nutrition Info:

Per Serving (½ cup): Calories: 116; Total fat: 2g; Protein: 7g; Total carbohydrate: 18g;

Conclusion

This 5-ingredient cookbook attempts to add something extra to the quick and simple dishes you cook frequently. When you peruse the recipes I have compiled for you, you will be inspired and be able to prepare them without making a special trip to the shop and spending a small fortune! Additionally, these dishes are not limited to families. They are ideal for someone who lives alone and must cook for himself daily, which might be a burden. These meals are also wonderful for newlyweds who have not cooked regularly since leaving their parents' home. The use of only five components allows you to save money. Your pantry will be loaded with all the required ingredients for your next tasty, time-efficient, cost-effective dinner when you buy intelligently. No one would know that you employed clever food-related techniques to fulfill your promise of having a delicious meal on the table by 7 p.m. every night.

Made in the USA
Monee, IL
24 November 2024